Fishing

Annette Smith

Illustrated by Karen Young

On Monday

I went fishing
with my mom.

3

On Tuesday

I went fishing
with my dad.

On Wednesday

I went fishing
with my big sister.

On Thursday

I went fishing
with my big brother.

On Friday

I went fishing
with my family.

On Saturday

I went fishing
with my grandma.

Look at my **fish!**

On Sunday

I went fishing
with my grandma again.